Breaking the Silence: Understanding and Overcoming Sexual Violence

C. P. Kumar
Reiki Healer
Roorkee - 247667, India

DEDICATION

This book is dedicated to all the survivors of sexual violence who have bravely shared their stories and inspired others to break the silence. Your courage, resilience, and strength have brought light to a dark issue and helped pave the way for change.

We also dedicate this book to the advocates, activists, and organizations who tirelessly work to end sexual violence and support survivors. Your dedication and commitment to this cause are invaluable and make a significant difference in the lives of many.

Finally, we dedicate this book to everyone who is willing to listen, learn, and take action. Only by working together can we create a world where sexual violence is no longer a prevalent issue.

C. P. Kumar

CONTENTS

PREFACE

Sexual violence is a pervasive problem that affects millions of people worldwide. It takes many forms, from sexual harassment and assault to rape, and has long-lasting and profound consequences for survivors. Despite its prevalence, sexual violence remains a taboo topic, shrouded in silence and stigma. Breaking the Silence: Understanding and Overcoming Sexual Violence aims to change that by providing a comprehensive and accessible guide to this complex and sensitive issue.

This book is intended for survivors of sexual violence, their loved ones, and anyone who wants to learn more about this important topic. It is also for professionals who work with survivors, such as counselors, therapists, lawyers, and healthcare providers.

Breaking the Silence covers a range of topics related to sexual violence, including understanding sexual harassment and rape, the psychological impact of sexual assault, healing from sexual trauma, and strategies for staying safe in a world of sexual violence. The book also explores the wider impact of sexual violence on society, including the consequences of sexual harassment and rape and the ways in which power dynamics can contribute to sexual harassment in the workplace.

In addition, Breaking the Silence provides guidance for survivors who choose to pursue legal action, including navigating the legal system and the challenges that survivors may face. It also delves into the psychology of sexual predators, examining the different types of offenders and the methods they use to groom and manipulate their victims.

Throughout the book, Breaking the Silence emphasizes the importance of consent and boundaries in all types of relationships and provides practical advice for staying safe in a world where sexual violence is all too common.

Breaking the Silence: Understanding and Overcoming Sexual Violence is a comprehensive guide that provides both information and hope for survivors of sexual violence. It is also a call to action for society as a whole to break the silence and work towards a world where sexual violence is no longer tolerated.

C. P. Kumar
Reiki Healer
Former Scientist 'G', National Institute of
Hydrology
Roorkee - 247667, India
E-mail: cpkumar@yahoo.com
https://www.angelfire.com/nh/cpkumar/virgo.html

Chapter 1. Breaking the Silence
Understanding Sexual Harassment and Rape

Introduction

Sexual harassment and rape are two of the most significant problems faced by women across the world. These issues have been prevalent for centuries and have affected women of all ages, races, and socio-economic backgrounds. Despite numerous efforts to combat sexual harassment and rape, they continue to occur, often without any consequences for the perpetrators. This article will explore sexual harassment and rape, their impact on individuals and society, and how we can take steps to address them.

Defining Sexual Harassment

Sexual harassment is defined as any unwanted sexual behavior, verbal or physical, that makes an individual feel uncomfortable, intimidated, or humiliated. Sexual harassment can take many forms, including unwanted touching, sexual comments, advances, and gestures, and the display of sexual images or content. Sexual harassment can occur in various settings, including the workplace, schools, social settings, and online.

Understanding Rape

Rape is a form of sexual assault that involves non-consensual sexual intercourse or penetration. It is a violent act that involves the use of physical force, threats, or coercion to force someone to engage in sexual activity. Rape can occur between strangers, acquaintances, or intimate partners, and it can have long-lasting effects on the victim, including physical, emotional, and psychological trauma.

The Impact of Sexual Harassment and Rape

Sexual harassment and rape have far-reaching consequences, not just for the individuals who experience them but also for society as a whole. Victims of sexual harassment and rape may experience a range of physical and emotional symptoms, including anxiety, depression, post-traumatic stress disorder (PTSD), and sexual dysfunction. Victims may also experience social and economic consequences, including job loss, loss of income, and difficulties forming and maintaining relationships.

Sexual harassment and rape also have broader societal impacts. They contribute to a culture of violence and discrimination against women, perpetuate gender inequality, and reinforce harmful gender stereotypes. Sexual harassment and rape are barriers to achieving gender equality and impede progress towards building a more just and equitable society.

Breaking the Silence

Breaking the silence surrounding sexual harassment and rape is an essential step towards addressing these issues. Victims of sexual harassment and rape often face shame, stigma, and fear when coming forward. They may fear retaliation from the perpetrator, doubt from others, or face victim-blaming attitudes. It is essential to create safe spaces for victims to share their experiences and seek support.

One way to break the silence is to encourage open and honest conversations about sexual harassment and rape. This includes challenging harmful gender stereotypes and norms, calling out inappropriate behavior, and promoting respect and consent in all forms of relationships. It also involves educating individuals about what constitutes sexual harassment and rape and the legal and ethical implications of engaging in these behaviors.

Preventing Sexual Harassment and Rape

Preventing sexual harassment and rape requires a comprehensive approach that addresses the root causes of these issues. This includes promoting gender equality and challenging harmful gender norms and stereotypes. It also involves creating safe and inclusive environments that promote respect, consent, and healthy relationships.

In the workplace, preventing sexual harassment requires clear policies and procedures for reporting and addressing sexual harassment, as well as training for employees on what constitutes sexual harassment and how to prevent it. Employers must take sexual harassment complaints seriously and take action to investigate and address them promptly.

In schools, preventing sexual harassment and rape requires comprehensive sex education that includes information on healthy relationships, consent, and sexual violence prevention. Schools must also have clear policies and procedures for reporting and addressing sexual harassment and provide support for victims.

In communities, preventing sexual harassment and rape requires a collective effort to promote respect and consent and challenge harmful gender stereotypes and norms. This includes supporting and funding organizations that work to prevent sexual harassment and rape, advocating for policy changes that protect victims and hold perpetrators accountable, and promoting awareness and education around these issues.

Supporting Victims of Sexual Harassment and Rape

Supporting victims of sexual harassment and rape is critical to addressing these issues. Victims of sexual harassment and rape often face significant barriers to reporting and seeking support, including shame, stigma, and fear of retaliation. Providing support and resources to victims can help them overcome these barriers and begin to heal from the trauma they have experienced.

Victims of sexual harassment and rape can seek support from a variety of sources, including friends and family, professional counselors and therapists, and advocacy organizations. Many organizations provide free and confidential support to victims of sexual harassment and rape, including crisis hotlines, counseling services, and legal assistance.

It is important to believe and support victims when they come forward with their experiences. Victims of sexual harassment and rape often face doubt and victim-blaming attitudes from others, which can exacerbate the trauma they have experienced. Supporting victims and taking their experiences seriously is essential to addressing sexual harassment and rape and promoting a culture of respect and consent.

Holding Perpetrators Accountable

Holding perpetrators accountable for sexual harassment and rape is essential to preventing these issues from occurring. Perpetrators of sexual harassment and rape often face few consequences for their actions, which can contribute to a culture of impunity and enable these behaviors to continue.

To hold perpetrators accountable, we must create a legal and social framework that prioritizes victim safety and well-being and punishes perpetrators for their actions. This includes creating laws and policies that protect victims from retaliation and provide them with the support they need to report and seek justice. It also involves promoting awareness and education around sexual harassment and rape, challenging harmful gender norms and stereotypes, and supporting victims in their pursuit of justice.

Conclusion

Sexual harassment and rape are complex issues that require a comprehensive and sustained effort to address. Breaking the silence around these issues, promoting respect and consent, and supporting victims and holding perpetrators accountable are essential steps towards building a more just and equitable society.

We must all play a role in preventing sexual harassment and rape, whether by challenging harmful gender norms and stereotypes, advocating for policy changes, supporting victims, or holding perpetrators accountable. By working together, we can create a culture that promotes respect, consent, and healthy relationships and eliminates sexual harassment and rape from our communities.

Introduction

Sexual assault is a traumatic event that can leave physical, emotional, and psychological scars on survivors. While physical injuries may heal with time and treatment, the emotional and psychological wounds of sexual assault can linger for years, impacting every aspect of a survivor's life. In this article, we will explore the psychological impact of sexual assault, including common symptoms and coping mechanisms, as well as resources available to survivors.

Defining Sexual Assault

Sexual assault is any unwanted sexual contact or activity that occurs without consent. This can include rape, molestation, sexual harassment, and other forms of non-consensual sexual activity. Sexual assault can happen to anyone, regardless of age, gender, sexual orientation, or race.

Psychological Impact of Sexual Assault

Sexual assault can have a profound impact on a survivor's mental health and wellbeing. The psychological effects of sexual assault can vary widely depending on factors such as the survivor's age, gender, and the nature of the assault. However, some common psychological symptoms experienced by survivors include:

1. Post-Traumatic Stress Disorder (PTSD)

PTSD is a mental health disorder that can develop after a person experiences or witnesses a traumatic event, such as sexual assault. Symptoms of PTSD can include flashbacks, nightmares, intrusive thoughts, and avoidance behaviors. Survivors of sexual assault may also experience hyperarousal, which can cause feelings of anxiety, panic, and hypervigilance.

2. Depression and Anxiety

Depression and anxiety are common psychological symptoms experienced by survivors of sexual assault. Survivors may feel overwhelmed, helpless, and hopeless, leading to feelings of sadness, worthlessness, and low self-esteem. Anxiety symptoms can include constant worry, fear, and nervousness, which can impact a survivor's ability to function in their daily life.

3. Substance Abuse

Survivors of sexual assault may turn to drugs or alcohol as a coping mechanism to deal with the emotional pain and trauma. Substance abuse can lead to addiction, which can further exacerbate psychological symptoms and make it harder for survivors to heal.

4. Self-Harm and Suicidal Thoughts

Survivors of sexual assault may experience intense feelings of shame, guilt, and self-blame. These feelings can lead to self-harm behaviors such as cutting, burning, or other forms of self-injury. Survivors may also experience suicidal thoughts, which can be a result of feeling overwhelmed by the trauma and the emotional pain that accompanies it.

5. Relationship Difficulties

Survivors of sexual assault may struggle with trust and intimacy in their relationships. They may have difficulty forming close relationships, fear intimacy, and struggle with communication. This can lead to social isolation, making it harder for survivors to heal and recover.

Coping Mechanisms for Survivors

Survivors of sexual assault may employ a variety of coping mechanisms to deal with the emotional and psychological effects of the trauma. Some common coping mechanisms include:

1. Therapy

Therapy can be an effective way for survivors of sexual assault to address the emotional and psychological impact of the trauma. Therapists can help survivors work through their feelings, develop coping strategies, and create a plan for healing and recovery.

2. Support Groups

Support groups can be a valuable resource for survivors of sexual assault. Survivors can connect with others who have had similar experiences, share their stories, and find support and understanding.

3. Self-Care

Self-care practices such as exercise, meditation, and relaxation techniques can help survivors manage stress, anxiety, and depression. Taking care of oneself physically, mentally, and emotionally can also help survivors feel empowered and in control.

4. Advocacy and Activism

Some survivors may find strength in advocacy and activism. Working to raise awareness about sexual assault, participating in marches or protests, and volunteering for organizations that support survivors can provide a sense of purpose and help survivors feel like they are making a difference.

5. Creative Expression

Creative expression such as art, writing, or music can be a powerful tool for survivors to process and express their emotions. Creative expression can help survivors feel more in control of their thoughts and feelings, and provide an outlet for their pain.

Resources for Survivors

Survivors of sexual assault can access a range of resources to help them cope with the emotional and psychological effects of the trauma. Some resources available to survivors include:

1. National Sexual Assault Hotline

The National Sexual Assault Hotline is available 24/7 to provide support and assistance to survivors of sexual assault. The hotline is staffed by trained advocates who can provide information, referrals, and crisis counseling.

2. Counseling and Therapy

Survivors can seek counseling and therapy from licensed mental health professionals who specialize in trauma and sexual assault. Therapy can be accessed through community mental health clinics, private practices, and organizations that provide services to survivors.

3. Support Groups

Survivors can connect with other survivors through local and online support groups.

Support groups provide a safe space for survivors to share their experiences, find support, and develop coping strategies.

4. Rape Crisis Centers

Rape crisis centers provide a range of services to survivors of sexual assault, including counseling, support groups, legal advocacy, and referrals to other resources.

5. Legal Assistance

Survivors may need legal assistance to obtain protective orders, seek justice, or address other legal issues related to the assault. Legal assistance can be obtained through organizations that specialize in providing legal services to survivors.

Conclusion

Sexual assault is a traumatic event that can have a profound impact on a survivor's mental health and wellbeing. Survivors may experience a range of psychological symptoms such as PTSD, depression, and anxiety, as well as self-harm behaviors, substance abuse, and relationship difficulties. However, there are resources available to help survivors cope with the emotional and psychological effects of the trauma, including therapy, support groups, self-care practices, advocacy, and creative expression. Survivors should know that they are not alone and that help is available to them.

Chapter 3. From Victim to Survivor

Healing from Sexual Trauma

Introduction

Sexual trauma is a deeply painful and traumatic experience that can have a long-lasting impact on a person's mental and emotional well-being. Survivors of sexual trauma often struggle with feelings of shame, guilt, and fear, and may find it difficult to trust others or form healthy relationships. However, with the right support and resources, it is possible for survivors to move from victimhood to survivorship and begin the healing process. In this article, we will explore the steps that survivors can take to heal from sexual trauma and regain their sense of control and autonomy.

Understanding Sexual Trauma

Sexual trauma can take many forms, including rape, sexual assault, sexual abuse, and sexual harassment. It is a violation of a person's boundaries and can leave them feeling helpless, powerless, and traumatized.

The experience of sexual trauma can have a profound impact on a person's mental health, leading to conditions such as anxiety, depression, post-traumatic stress disorder (PTSD), and borderline personality disorder.

One of the most challenging aspects of sexual trauma is the shame and stigma that often accompanies it. Survivors may blame themselves for what happened or feel that others will judge them for what they have experienced. It is essential to understand that sexual trauma is never the survivor's fault, and there is no shame in seeking help and support to heal from the trauma.

Seeking Support

One of the most important steps that survivors can take towards healing is to seek support. This can include reaching out to friends and family members who are supportive and understanding, as well as seeking professional help from therapists or counselors who specialize in working with survivors of sexual trauma.

Support groups can also be a valuable resource for survivors, providing a safe and non-judgmental space to share their experiences and connect with others who have been through similar trauma. Online support groups and forums can also be a helpful resource for survivors who may not have access to in-person support groups.

It is important to find a support system that works for the individual survivor, as everyone's needs and experiences are unique. What works for one person may not work for another, and it may take some trial and error to find the right support system.

Working Through the Trauma

Working through the trauma of sexual trauma can be a long and challenging process, but it is an essential step towards healing. This may involve working with a therapist or counselor to process the trauma and develop coping strategies to manage the emotional and psychological impact of the trauma.

Some common therapeutic approaches for working through sexual trauma include cognitive-behavioral therapy (CBT), eye movement desensitization and reprocessing (EMDR), and trauma-focused therapy. These approaches focus on helping survivors to process their trauma and develop healthy coping mechanisms to manage the emotional and psychological impact of the trauma.

Self-Care and Coping Strategies

Self-care and coping strategies are essential tools for survivors of sexual trauma, helping them to manage the emotional and psychological impact of the trauma and regain a sense of control and autonomy. Coping strategies may include mindfulness practices, such as meditation or yoga, as well as physical activities like exercise or sports.

It is also important for survivors to prioritize their physical health, including eating a healthy diet, getting enough sleep, and avoiding drugs and alcohol, which can exacerbate the emotional and psychological impact of the trauma. Engaging in creative pursuits, such as art or music, can also be a valuable coping mechanism for survivors, providing an outlet for self-expression and emotional release.

Setting Boundaries and Rebuilding Trust

Sexual trauma can leave survivors feeling vulnerable and distrustful of others, making it challenging to form healthy relationships and set boundaries. It is essential for survivors to take the time to rebuild their trust in themselves and others, and to establish healthy boundaries to protect themselves from further harm.

This may involve setting clear boundaries with friends, family, and romantic partners, and learning to say no when something feels uncomfortable or triggering. It can also involve developing a greater sense of self-awareness and learning to listen to one's own needs and intuition.

Rebuilding trust can be a challenging process, but it is possible with the right support and resources. This may involve working with a therapist or counselor to develop healthy relationship patterns and communication skills, as well as engaging in activities that promote trust and connection with others, such as volunteering or participating in group activities.

Finding Meaning and Purpose

One of the most important aspects of healing from sexual trauma is finding meaning and purpose in life beyond the trauma. This may involve exploring new interests and hobbies, pursuing educational or career goals, or engaging in activism or advocacy work related to sexual assault and trauma.

By finding meaning and purpose beyond the trauma, survivors can begin to reclaim their sense of self and autonomy, and move towards a brighter and more fulfilling future. It is important for survivors to remember that healing is a journey, and that there is no set timeline or "right" way to heal. With the right support and resources, survivors can move from victimhood to survivorship, and begin to live a life that is meaningful, purposeful, and fulfilling.

The Importance of Self-Compassion

Throughout the healing journey, it is important for survivors of sexual trauma to practice self-compassion. This means treating oneself with kindness and understanding, and recognizing that healing is a difficult and challenging process that takes time.

Self-compassion can involve engaging in positive self-talk, practicing self-care and self-nurturing behaviors, and being patient and gentle with oneself. By practicing self-compassion, survivors can begin to let go of feelings of shame and self-blame, and move towards a greater sense of self-acceptance and self-love.

Moving Forward: Life After Trauma

Healing from sexual trauma is not a linear process, and it is common for survivors to experience setbacks and triggers along the way. However, with the right support and resources, survivors can move towards a brighter future and reclaim their sense of self and autonomy.

It is important for survivors to remember that healing is a journey, and that it takes time, patience, and self-compassion. By seeking support, working through the trauma, practicing self-care and coping strategies, setting boundaries and rebuilding trust, finding meaning and purpose, and practicing self-compassion, survivors can move from victimhood to survivorship, and begin to live a life that is fulfilling and meaningful.

Conclusion

Sexual trauma is a deeply painful and traumatic experience that can have a long-lasting impact on a person's mental and emotional well-being. However, with the right support and resources, survivors can move from victimhood to survivorship, and begin the healing process.

By seeking support, working through the trauma, practicing self-care and coping strategies, setting boundaries and rebuilding trust, finding meaning and purpose, and practicing self-compassion, survivors can begin to reclaim their sense of self and autonomy, and move towards a brighter and more fulfilling future.

It is important for survivors to remember that healing is a journey, and that there is no set timeline or "right" way to heal. With the right support and resources, survivors can begin to live a life that is meaningful, purposeful, and fulfilling, and move towards a brighter future beyond the trauma.

Introduction

The #MeToo movement has brought the issue of sexual harassment and assault to the forefront of public discourse. It has encouraged people to speak out about their experiences and has led to a greater awareness of the prevalence of these issues. However, there is still much to be done in terms of addressing and preventing sexual harassment and assault. This guide aims to provide a comprehensive overview of sexual harassment and rape, including definitions, statistics, and resources for victims.

What is Sexual Harassment?

Sexual harassment is a form of discrimination that involves unwanted sexual advances, requests for sexual favors, or other verbal or physical conduct of a sexual nature. It can occur in a variety of settings, including the workplace, schools, and public spaces. Sexual harassment can also take the form of non-verbal behavior, such as staring or leering.

Sexual harassment can be divided into two categories: quid pro quo and hostile environment. Quid pro quo harassment involves a situation where a person in a position of power offers rewards or threatens negative consequences in exchange for sexual favors. Hostile environment harassment refers to an environment in which sexual conduct or comments create an intimidating, hostile, or offensive atmosphere.

Statistics on Sexual Harassment

Sexual harassment is a widespread problem that affects people of all genders, ages, and backgrounds. According to a 2018 survey by the Pew Research Center, 59% of women and 27% of men in the United States reported experiencing some form of sexual harassment. The same survey found that women of color, LGBTQ+ individuals, and people with disabilities are more likely to experience sexual harassment than their counterparts.

What is Rape?

Rape is a form of sexual assault that involves non-consensual sexual activity. This can include vaginal, anal, or oral penetration, as well as other forms of sexual contact. Rape is a serious crime that can have long-lasting physical and psychological effects on victims.

Statistics on Rape

Rape is a serious and widespread problem that affects people of all genders. According to the National Sexual Violence Resource Center, one in five women and one in 71 men in the United States will experience rape at some point in their lives. The same organization reports that transgender individuals are at an even higher risk of experiencing rape, with 47% of transgender individuals experiencing sexual assault in their lifetimes.

Preventing Sexual Harassment and Rape

Preventing sexual harassment and rape requires a multifaceted approach that involves education, policy changes, and cultural shifts. Some strategies for preventing sexual harassment and rape include:

1. Education: Providing education on consent, healthy relationships, and bystander intervention can help to prevent sexual harassment and rape. Education should be provided at all levels, from elementary school through college and beyond.

2. Policy Changes: Implementing policies that prohibit sexual harassment and rape, and providing training for employees and students on these policies, can help to prevent these issues from occurring. Policies should include clear definitions of sexual harassment and rape, reporting procedures, and consequences for perpetrators.

3. Cultural Shifts: Changing cultural attitudes towards sexual harassment and rape can help to prevent these issues from occurring. This includes challenging harmful stereotypes and beliefs about gender and sexuality, and promoting a culture of respect and consent.

Resources for Victims

If you or someone you know has experienced sexual harassment or rape, it is important to seek help and support. There are many resources available for victims, including:

1. National Sexual Assault Hotline: The National Sexual Assault Hotline provides free, confidential support to survivors of sexual assault. The hotline is available 24/7 and can be reached at 1-800-656-HOPE (4673).

2. RAINN: The Rape, Abuse & Incest National Network (RAINN) is the largest anti-sexual violence organization in the United States and provides a range of resources for victims, including a hotline, online chat, and local support services. Their website, rainn.org, also provides information on reporting sexual assault and finding a healthcare provider.

3. Local Resources: Many cities and states have local organizations that provide support and resources for victims of sexual harassment and rape. These organizations may offer counseling, legal support, and advocacy services. You can search for local resources using the National Sexual Violence Resource Center's directory.

4. Therapy: Therapy can be a helpful resource for survivors of sexual harassment and rape. A therapist can provide support, help with processing emotions, and develop coping strategies. It is important to find a therapist who has experience working with survivors of sexual trauma.

Reporting Sexual Harassment and Rape

Reporting sexual harassment and rape can be a difficult and complex process, but it is an important step towards justice and accountability. If you have experienced sexual harassment or rape, there are several options for reporting:

1. Law Enforcement: You can report sexual harassment and rape to law enforcement. This can involve filing a police report, cooperating with an investigation, and potentially testifying in court. It is important to remember that the criminal justice system can be challenging for survivors and may not always result in a conviction.

2. Employer or School: If you have experienced sexual harassment in the workplace or at school, you can report it to your employer or school. Employers and schools are required to investigate reports of

sexual harassment and take appropriate action.

3. Title IX: Title IX is a federal law that prohibits discrimination on the basis of sex in education programs and activities. This includes sexual harassment and rape. If you have experienced sexual harassment or rape at a school, you can file a complaint with the school's Title IX coordinator.

Conclusion

Sexual harassment and rape are serious issues that require a comprehensive and multifaceted approach to prevention and response. Education, policy changes, and cultural shifts are all necessary components of this approach. If you or someone you know has experienced sexual harassment or rape, it is important to seek help and support from a trained professional or organization. Reporting sexual harassment and rape can be difficult, but it is an important step towards accountability and justice. Together, we can work towards creating a world where sexual harassment and rape are no longer tolerated.

Introduction

In recent years, there has been a growing awareness of the importance of consent and boundaries in interpersonal relationships. Consent is the enthusiastic and voluntary agreement to engage in sexual activity, and it is an essential component of healthy sexual relationships. Boundaries are the limits that individuals set for themselves in their relationships, and they are crucial for maintaining emotional and physical safety. In this article, we will explore the concept of consent and boundaries, why they are important, and how to understand and respect them.

What is Consent?

Consent is the affirmative, enthusiastic, and voluntary agreement to engage in sexual activity. It is essential to obtain consent before engaging in any sexual activity. It means that both parties have freely and consciously agreed to participate in sexual activity without coercion or pressure from the other party. Consent must be given before every sexual act, and it can be withdrawn at any time. Silence, lack of resistance, or being under the influence of drugs or alcohol does not constitute consent.

Understanding Boundaries

Boundaries are the limits that individuals set for themselves in their relationships. They are the physical, emotional, and psychological limits that help individuals feel safe and respected. Setting boundaries involves understanding and communicating one's needs and desires, as well as respecting the boundaries of others. Boundaries can vary depending on the individual and the relationship, but they are always important to establish and respect.

Why Consent and Boundaries are Important

Consent and boundaries are essential for creating healthy and fulfilling relationships. Without consent, sexual activity can be harmful and traumatic for the person who did not give their consent. Without boundaries, individuals may feel disrespected, ignored, or taken advantage of in their relationships. Consensual relationships that respect each other's boundaries are much more likely to be satisfying, safe, and fulfilling for both parties.

Misconceptions About Consent

There are many misconceptions about consent that can lead to confusion and harm. One common misconception is that a person can give consent to sexual activity when they are under the influence of drugs or alcohol. In reality, a person who is intoxicated cannot give meaningful consent because they may not be able to understand the consequences of their actions. Another common misconception is that once a person has given consent, they cannot change their mind. In reality, consent can be withdrawn at any time, and respecting a person's decision to change their mind is essential.

How to Respect Boundaries

Respecting boundaries involves understanding and communicating one's own needs and desires, as well as respecting the boundaries of others. Here are some tips for respecting boundaries in relationships:

1. Communicate: Communicate clearly and openly with your partner about your boundaries and expectations. Be honest about what you are comfortable with and what you are not comfortable with.

2. Listen: Listen actively to your partner's needs and desires, and respect their boundaries. Avoid pressuring your partner to engage in activities they are not comfortable with.

3. Be Mindful: Be mindful of body language and verbal cues that suggest your partner is uncomfortable or hesitant. If your partner seems uncomfortable, ask if they are okay and respect their response.

4. Check-In: Check-in with your partner regularly to ensure that their boundaries are being respected. Encourage them to speak up if they feel their boundaries are being crossed.

5. Respect: Finally, always respect your partner's boundaries, even if they are different from your own. Boundaries are essential for maintaining emotional and physical safety in relationships.

How to Obtain Consent

Obtaining consent involves asking for and receiving enthusiastic and voluntary agreement to engage in sexual activity. Here are some tips for obtaining consent:

1. Ask: Ask your partner for their consent before engaging in any sexual activity. Be clear about what you are asking for and what you are comfortable with.

2. Listen: Listen actively to your partner's response. If they hesitate or seem unsure, stop and ask if they are okay or if there is anything they want to talk about.

3. Respect: Respect your partner's response, whether it is a yes or a no. If they say no, do not pressure them or try to change their mind.

4. Check-In: Check-in with your partner throughout the sexual activity to ensure that their consent is ongoing. Encourage them to speak up if they become uncomfortable or if their boundaries are being crossed.

5. Non-Verbal Cues: Pay attention to non-verbal cues, such as body language and facial expressions, to ensure that your

partner is comfortable and enthusiastic about the sexual activity.

Consent and the Law

Consent is an essential component of healthy sexual relationships, and it is also a legal requirement. In many countries, sexual activity without consent is considered sexual assault or rape, and it is a criminal offense. It is important to understand the laws regarding consent in your country or state and to ensure that all sexual activity is consensual and legal.

Consent and Power Dynamics

Power dynamics can play a significant role in consent and boundaries in relationships. In some cases, individuals may feel pressure to engage in sexual activity due to power imbalances, such as age differences, status differences, or authority figures. It is important to be aware of power imbalances in relationships and to ensure that all sexual activity is voluntary and consensual.

Consent and Sexual Violence

Sexual violence is a serious issue that affects millions of people around the world. Sexual violence can occur in any relationship, regardless of gender, age, or sexual orientation. It is important to understand the signs of sexual violence and to seek help if you or someone you know is experiencing it. Sexual violence can have long-lasting effects on individuals and their relationships, and it is essential to take it seriously and seek support.

Conclusion

Consent and boundaries are essential components of healthy relationships, and they are crucial for maintaining emotional and physical safety. It is important to understand the concept of consent and to obtain it before engaging in any sexual activity. Setting and respecting boundaries is also important for maintaining respectful and fulfilling relationships. By understanding and respecting consent and boundaries, we can create a safer and more fulfilling world for all.

Chapter 6. The Dark Side of Power

Examining Sexual Harassment in the Workplace

Introduction

Sexual harassment is a pervasive and damaging problem that continues to afflict workplaces around the world. Despite efforts to combat it, it remains a serious issue that affects individuals, organizations, and societies. Sexual harassment can take many forms, but at its core, it is about the abuse of power. In this article, we will examine the dark side of power and explore the nature and impact of sexual harassment in the workplace.

Defining Sexual Harassment in the Workplace

Sexual harassment is a form of sex discrimination that involves unwelcome sexual advances, requests for sexual favors, or other verbal or physical conduct of a sexual nature. The behavior can be explicit or implicit, and it can occur between people of different or the same gender. Sexual harassment can take many forms, including but not limited to:

- ❖ Verbal harassment, such as sexual jokes, comments, or propositions.
- ❖ Physical harassment, such as touching, groping, or assault.
- ❖ Visual harassment, such as displaying sexually suggestive images or objects.
- ❖ Psychological harassment, such as belittling or humiliating comments or gestures.

It is important to note that sexual harassment is not limited to interactions between co-workers. It can also involve behavior by supervisors, managers, or other people with power in the workplace.

The Impact of Sexual Harassment

Sexual harassment can have severe and lasting effects on individuals and organizations. Victims of sexual harassment may experience a range of negative consequences, including:

- ➢ Emotional distress, such as anxiety, depression, and post-traumatic stress disorder.

- ➢ Physical symptoms, such as headaches, stomach problems, and sleep disturbances.
- ➢ Reduced job satisfaction and motivation.
- ➢ Loss of confidence and self-esteem.
- ➢ Career setbacks, such as being passed over for promotions or being terminated.

The impact of sexual harassment can also extend beyond the individual to affect the organization as a whole. Sexual harassment can create a toxic work environment that undermines productivity, erodes trust, and damages the reputation of the organization. It can also lead to increased turnover and absenteeism, as well as legal and financial liabilities.

The Dark Side of Power

Sexual harassment is fundamentally about the abuse of power. It occurs when someone with power in the workplace, such as a supervisor or manager, uses that power to coerce or intimidate someone with less power, such as a subordinate or colleague. This power dynamic can make it difficult for victims to speak out or take action, as they may fear retaliation or damage to their careers. The abuse of power can take many forms, including:

- Using threats or intimidation to coerce someone into sexual behavior.
- Offering job benefits, such as promotions or raises, in exchange for sexual favors.
- Punishing someone who rejects sexual advances, such as by denying them opportunities or giving them poor evaluations.
- Creating a hostile work environment through sexually explicit language or behavior.

These actions can be particularly damaging when they are committed by someone in a position of authority, as it can create a culture of fear and silence that allows sexual harassment to continue unchecked.

Preventing and Addressing Sexual Harassment

Preventing and addressing sexual harassment in the workplace requires a multifaceted approach that involves education, training, and strong policies and procedures. Employers can take a number of steps to create a workplace that is free from sexual harassment, including:

- Establishing clear policies and procedures for addressing sexual harassment.
- Providing regular training for employees and supervisors on what constitutes sexual harassment and how to prevent it.
- Encouraging employees to report incidents of sexual harassment and providing multiple avenues for doing so.
- Investigating and addressing all reports of sexual harassment promptly and thoroughly.
- Implementing consequences for those who engage in sexual harassment, including termination, when appropriate.
- Creating a culture of respect and inclusivity that values diversity and promotes a safe and respectful work environment.

Conclusion

Sexual harassment in the workplace is a serious problem that can have lasting effects on individuals, organizations, and society as a whole. It is fundamentally about the abuse of power, and preventing and addressing it requires a concerted effort by employers, employees, and society as a whole. By taking a multifaceted approach that includes education, training, and strong policies and procedures, we can create a workplace that is free from sexual harassment and that promotes a culture of respect and inclusivity.

It is important to remember that sexual harassment is not just a workplace issue, but a societal issue. It is a reflection of broader power imbalances and systemic inequalities that exist in our society. Addressing sexual harassment requires not only addressing the individual incidents, but also addressing the underlying causes of these incidents. This means working to create a more just and equitable society that values diversity, promotes inclusion, and provides equal opportunities for all.

In conclusion, sexual harassment in the workplace is a serious problem that requires a collective effort to address. By acknowledging the dark side of power and working to create a workplace culture that is free from sexual harassment, we can create a safer and more inclusive workplace for everyone. It is time to take action and make sure that sexual harassment is no longer tolerated in any workplace.

Introduction

Sexual offenses are one of the most heinous crimes that society faces today. Sexual predators or offenders often pose a significant threat to vulnerable individuals, including children and women. While it's important to hold these individuals accountable for their actions, it's also essential to understand the psychology behind their behavior. In this article, we will delve into the world of sexual predators, their motivations, and the psychological factors that drive their behavior.

Understanding the Offender

Sexual predators can be anyone, from family members to strangers, but they all share a common trait: the desire to exert power and control over their victims. They use sexual violence as a tool to assert dominance and gain a sense of power over their victims. However, not all sexual predators have the same motivations or behavioral patterns.

Psychologists have identified several types of sexual offenders based on their behavior patterns and motivations.

Types of Sexual Predators

1. Power-Oriented Sexual Predators

Power-oriented sexual predators are individuals who derive pleasure from exerting power and control over their victims. They often target vulnerable individuals, such as children or those with disabilities, because they perceive them as easy targets. These offenders often use physical violence or threats to achieve their goals and may even plan their attacks in advance.

2. Anger-Excitation Sexual Predators

Anger-excitation sexual predators are individuals who use sexual violence as a way to channel their anger and aggression. They may have a history of violence, and their attacks are often impulsive and unplanned. These offenders often have a history of domestic violence or other forms of violent behavior.

3. Sadistic Sexual Predators

Sadistic sexual predators are individuals who derive pleasure from inflicting pain or humiliation on their victims. They often have a history of animal cruelty or other forms of violent behavior. These offenders may also have a fascination with weapons or bondage and may use these tools to inflict harm on their victims.

4. Opportunistic Sexual Predators

Opportunistic sexual predators are individuals who take advantage of situations where their victims are vulnerable. For example, they may target individuals who are intoxicated or alone in isolated areas. These offenders often do not plan their attacks in advance and may not have a specific victim in mind.

Psychological Factors

While the motivations of sexual predators vary, there are several psychological factors that are common among them. These factors may include:

1. Childhood Trauma

Many sexual predators have experienced childhood trauma, including physical or sexual abuse. This trauma can lead to feelings of powerlessness and a desire for control over others, which may manifest in their sexual behavior.

2. Distorted Thinking Patterns

Sexual predators often have distorted thinking patterns that justify their behavior. For example, they may believe that their victims are willing participants or that their actions are not harmful. These beliefs allow them to rationalize their behavior and continue to engage in sexual violence.

3. Lack of Empathy

Sexual predators often lack empathy for their victims and may not recognize the harm that they are causing. They may view their victims as objects to be used for their own pleasure, rather than as human beings with feelings and emotions.

Some sexual predators may have personality disorders, such as narcissistic personality disorder or antisocial personality disorder. These disorders can lead to a lack of empathy and a desire for power and control over others.

Preventing Sexual Violence

Preventing sexual violence requires a multifaceted approach that addresses both the individual and societal factors that contribute to sexual violence. Some of the strategies that may be effective in preventing sexual violence include:

1. Education

Educating individuals about consent and healthy sexual relationships can help to prevent sexual violence. This education should begin at a young age and should include information about healthy relationships, boundaries, and consent.

2. Empowerment

Empowering victims to speak out and report sexual violence can also be an effective prevention strategy. This can be achieved through providing support services and resources for victims, as well as creating safe and supportive environments where victims feel comfortable speaking out.

3. Addressing Societal Factors

Addressing societal factors that contribute to sexual violence, such as gender inequality and rape culture, can also be an effective prevention strategy. This requires a broader cultural shift that involves challenging harmful attitudes and beliefs about gender, sexuality, and power.

4. Treatment for Offenders

Providing treatment for sexual offenders can help to reduce the likelihood of reoffending. This treatment may include cognitive-behavioral therapy, which helps offenders to address their distorted thinking patterns, or medication to manage underlying mental health conditions.

Conclusion

Sexual violence is a complex issue that requires a nuanced understanding of the psychological factors that drive offender behavior. While it's important to hold sexual offenders accountable for their actions, it's also essential to understand the root causes of their behavior and to address the societal and individual factors that contribute to sexual violence. By taking a comprehensive approach to preventing sexual violence, we can work towards a future where all individuals are free from the threat of sexual violence.

Introduction

Sexual assault is a traumatic experience that can have a significant impact on a person's life. The legal system is one avenue that survivors of sexual assault can pursue to seek justice and hold perpetrators accountable for their actions. However, navigating the legal system as a sexual assault survivor can be challenging and overwhelming. This article aims to provide a guide on how survivors can navigate the legal system and seek legal justice.

Understanding the Legal System

The legal system is complex, and understanding it is crucial for survivors seeking legal justice. The legal system is composed of several components, including law enforcement, the court system, and attorneys. Law enforcement agencies are responsible for investigating crimes and gathering evidence, while the court system is responsible for determining whether a person is guilty or innocent. Attorneys are trained professionals who help survivors navigate the legal system and represent them in court.

Reporting Sexual Assault

Reporting sexual assault is the first step in seeking legal justice. Survivors can report sexual assault to law enforcement agencies, such as the police department or the sheriff's office. When reporting sexual assault, survivors should provide as much information as possible, including the date and time of the assault, the location of the assault, and a description of the perpetrator. Survivors should also seek medical attention, even if they do not have any physical injuries, as the medical report can serve as evidence in court.

Investigating Sexual Assault

After reporting sexual assault, law enforcement agencies will conduct an investigation. The investigation process can take some time, and survivors should be patient and cooperate with law enforcement officers. Survivors should provide any additional information or evidence that they may have, including photographs or videos of the assault, witness statements, or any other evidence that can help investigators.

Working with an Attorney

Survivors of sexual assault should work with an attorney who specializes in sexual assault cases. Attorneys can provide legal advice, represent survivors in court, and help survivors navigate the legal system. When selecting an attorney, survivors should look for someone who has experience handling sexual assault cases, understands the survivor's needs, and is compassionate and understanding.

Filing a Lawsuit

Survivors of sexual assault can file a lawsuit against the perpetrator. The lawsuit can seek compensation for damages, such as medical expenses, lost wages, and emotional distress. Survivors can also seek punitive damages, which are intended to punish the perpetrator for their actions. Filing a lawsuit can be a lengthy and challenging process, and survivors should work closely with their attorney throughout the process.

Attending Court Hearings

Survivors of sexual assault will need to attend court hearings as part of the legal process. Survivors should be prepared to testify in court and provide any additional information or evidence that may be necessary. Survivors can also request that certain accommodations be made to ensure their comfort and safety, such as a closed courtroom or a support person present during the hearing.

Dealing with Trauma

Navigating the legal system as a sexual assault survivor can be traumatic, and survivors should take steps to care for their emotional and mental well-being. Survivors can seek therapy or counseling to help them cope with the trauma of the assault and the legal process. Survivors can also join support groups or connect with other survivors to find emotional support and solidarity.

Conclusion

Seeking legal justice as a sexual assault survivor can be a daunting and overwhelming process, but it is an important step towards healing and holding perpetrators accountable for their actions. Survivors should educate themselves about the legal system, work with experienced attorneys, and take care of their emotional well-being throughout the process. While the legal system is not perfect, it can provide a sense of closure and justice for survivors of sexual assault.

Introduction

Sexual harassment and rape are heinous crimes that not only harm the victim but also create a ripple effect throughout society. These acts have far-reaching consequences that go beyond the immediate physical and emotional trauma suffered by the victim. In this article, we will explore the ripple effect of sexual harassment and rape, including its impact on the victim, their family and friends, society, and even the perpetrator themselves.

The Impact on the Victim

The impact of sexual harassment and rape on the victim is profound and long-lasting. Victims may suffer physical injuries, such as bruises, cuts, and broken bones, as well as psychological trauma. The psychological effects of sexual harassment and rape can include depression, anxiety, PTSD, and low self-esteem. Victims may also experience feelings of shame, guilt, and anger, which can affect their ability to trust others and form healthy relationships.

The Impact on Family and Friends

Sexual harassment and rape can also have a significant impact on the victim's family and friends. Loved ones may experience a range of emotions, including anger, guilt, and helplessness. They may also feel the need to provide emotional support to the victim, which can be emotionally taxing and time-consuming. In some cases, family and friends may also suffer from secondary trauma, which is a type of trauma that results from being exposed to another person's trauma.

The Impact on Society

Sexual harassment and rape also have a ripple effect on society as a whole. These crimes can create a culture of fear and mistrust, which can lead to a breakdown in social cohesion. Sexual harassment and rape can also contribute to gender-based violence and perpetuate harmful stereotypes about women and men. Moreover, the economic cost of sexual harassment and rape can be staggering, including the loss of productivity and the cost of healthcare and legal fees.

The Impact on Perpetrators

The impact of sexual harassment and rape is not limited to the victim and their loved ones. Perpetrators of these crimes can also suffer consequences, both legal and personal. Perpetrators may face criminal charges, fines, and imprisonment. They may also experience social ostracism, loss of employment, and damage to their reputation. Moreover, perpetrators may suffer from their own psychological trauma, including guilt, shame, and remorse.

Preventing Sexual Harassment and Rape

Preventing sexual harassment and rape is essential to reducing the ripple effect of these crimes. Prevention efforts should focus on promoting healthy relationships, respect for boundaries, and gender equality. Education about consent, healthy communication, and conflict resolution should also be part of prevention efforts. Organizations should have clear policies and procedures for addressing sexual harassment and rape, including reporting mechanisms, investigation protocols, and support services for victims.

Conclusion

Sexual harassment and rape have far-reaching consequences that go beyond the victim and their loved ones. These crimes can create a ripple effect that affects society as a whole. Preventing sexual harassment and rape is essential to reducing the impact of these crimes. Prevention efforts should focus on promoting healthy relationships, respect for boundaries, and gender equality. Organizations should also have clear policies and procedures for addressing sexual harassment and rape, including reporting mechanisms, investigation protocols, and support services for victims. By working together to prevent sexual harassment and rape, we can create a safer, more equitable society for everyone.

Introduction

Sexual violence is a pervasive and disturbing issue that affects people of all genders, ages, and backgrounds. It is a form of violence that is often shrouded in silence, shame, and stigma, making it challenging for survivors to seek support and justice. According to the World Health Organization (WHO), at least 1 in 3 women and girls worldwide experience some form of sexual violence in their lifetime. This statistic highlights the urgent need for effective strategies to prevent and respond to sexual violence. In this article, we will explore some of the ways that individuals can stay safe and protect themselves from sexual violence.

Understanding Sexual Violence

Before we discuss strategies for staying safe, it is essential to understand what sexual violence is and how it can manifest. Sexual violence is any form of unwanted sexual activity that is perpetrated against a person's will. This can include rape, sexual assault, sexual harassment, and unwanted touching or groping. Sexual violence can occur in a variety of settings, including the home, workplace, schools, and public spaces. It is often committed by someone the survivor knows, such as a partner, family member, friend, or acquaintance.

Sexual violence is a traumatic experience that can have significant and long-lasting effects on survivors' mental, physical, and emotional health. Survivors may experience symptoms such as anxiety, depression, post-traumatic stress disorder (PTSD), and substance abuse. It is essential to seek support if you have experienced sexual violence or know someone who has.

Strategies for Staying Safe

While sexual violence is a widespread problem, there are steps individuals can take to reduce their risk of experiencing it. The following are some strategies for staying safe in a world of sexual violence.

1. Trust Your Gut

One of the most important strategies for staying safe is to trust your instincts. If something feels off or uncomfortable, listen to your body and remove yourself from the situation. This could mean leaving a party, saying no to a date, or declining an invitation to go somewhere with someone you don't know well. If you feel unsafe in a situation, it's essential to prioritize your own well-being over social pressure or expectations.

2. Set Boundaries

Setting clear boundaries is another crucial strategy for staying safe. Communicate your limits to others, and don't be afraid to say no if you feel uncomfortable or unsafe. Boundaries can look different for everyone, so it's essential to identify what feels right for you. This could mean setting limits around physical touch, socializing in certain settings, or sharing personal information.

3. Practice Assertiveness

Being assertive can help you communicate your boundaries effectively and reduce the risk of being taken advantage of.

"Breaking the Silence: Understanding and Overcoming Sexual Violence" is a comprehensive guide that sheds light on the issue of sexual violence and its impact on survivors. The book covers a wide range of topics, including the different forms of sexual violence, the psychological impact of sexual assault, healing from trauma, understanding consent and boundaries, sexual harassment in the workplace, the psychology of sexual predators, navigating the legal system as a survivor, the ripple effect of sexual violence, and strategies for staying safe. The book provides a deep understanding of the issue and offers practical advice for survivors, their loved ones, and anyone who wants to help end sexual violence.

Assertiveness involves speaking up for yourself and expressing your needs and wants clearly and confidently. It can be challenging to be assertive, especially in situations where you feel vulnerable or threatened. However, practicing assertiveness can help you feel more empowered and in control of your own safety.

4. Stay Aware of Your Surroundings

Staying aware of your surroundings is another important strategy for staying safe. This involves paying attention to the people, places, and situations around you and being alert to any potential risks. For example, if you're walking alone at night, stay in well-lit areas and avoid using headphones that could distract you from your surroundings. If you're in a public space, be aware of who is around you and trust your instincts if you feel uneasy.

5. Use Technology Wisely

Technology can be a useful tool for staying connected and informed, but it can also increase the risk of sexual violence. Cyberbullying, revenge porn, and online grooming are all forms of sexual violence that can occur through technology. It's essential to use technology wisely and be mindful of the information you share online. Consider using privacy settings on social media platforms and avoiding sharing personal information with people you don't know well. If you receive unwanted or threatening messages or images, it's important to report them to the appropriate authorities.

6. Learn Self-Defense

Learning self-defense can be an effective way to protect yourself and feel more confident in potentially dangerous situations. Self-defense classes can teach you techniques for protecting yourself against physical assault and strategies for avoiding or de-escalating violent situations. Many community centers, gyms, and martial arts studios offer self-defense classes, and some classes specifically cater to women and LGBTQ+ individuals.

7. Seek Support

If you have experienced sexual violence or know someone who has, it's essential to seek support. This could include talking to a trusted friend or family member, seeking counseling or therapy, or reporting violence to law enforcement. There are many organizations that provide support resources for survivors of sexual violen such as hotlines, support groups, advocacy organizations.

Conclusion

Sexual violence is a complex and challenging issue that affects millions o people worldwide. While there is no surefire way to prevent sexual violence, there are strategies individuals can use to stay safe and protect themselves. Trusting your instincts, setting boundaries, practicing assertiveness, staying aware of your surroundings, using technology wisely, learning self-defense, and seeking support are all important strategies for staying safe in a world of sexual violence. It's important to remember that no one deserves to experience sexual violence, and support and resources are available for survivors. By working together to raise awareness, prevent sexual violence, and support survivors, we can create a safer and more just world for all.

counseling or therapy, or reporting the violence to law enforcement. There are also many organizations that provide support and resources for survivors of sexual violence, such as hotlines, support groups, and advocacy organizations.

Conclusion

Sexual violence is a complex and challenging issue that affects millions of people worldwide. While there is no surefire way to prevent sexual violence, there are strategies individuals can use to stay safe and protect themselves. Trusting your instincts, setting boundaries, practicing assertiveness, staying aware of your surroundings, using technology wisely, learning self-defense, and seeking support are all important strategies for staying safe in a world of sexual violence. It's important to remember that no one deserves to experience sexual violence, and support and resources are available for survivors. By working together to raise awareness, prevent sexual violence, and support survivors, we can create a safer and more just world for all.

"Breaking the Silence: Understanding and Overcoming Sexual Violence" is a comprehensive guide that sheds light on the issue of sexual violence and its impact on survivors. The book covers a wide range of topics, including the different forms of sexual violence, the psychological impact of sexual assault, healing from trauma, understanding consent and boundaries, sexual harassment in the workplace, the psychology of sexual predators, navigating the legal system as a survivor, the ripple effect of sexual violence, and strategies for staying safe. The book provides a deep understanding of the issue and offers practical advice for survivors, their loved ones, and anyone who wants to help end sexual violence.

ABOUT THE AUTHOR

Mr. C. P. Kumar is a retired Scientist 'G' from the National Institute of Hydrology, Roorkee, Uttarakhand, India. With a wealth of experience in his field, he has also been practicing alternative healing therapies for several years. He is skilled in Reiki Healing and Chakra Balancing with Pendulum Dowsing, and offers holistic therapy through Emotional Freedom Technique (EFT) for emotional issues. You can email Mr. Kumar at cpkumar@yahoo.com and also visit his Reiki blog at https://reiki-roorkee.blogspot.com/ for more information.

www.ingramcontent.com/pod-product-compliance
Lightning Source LLC
Chambersburg PA
CBHW050602160726
48003CB00003B/1016